THE AMERICAN SADDLEBRED

CONTENTS

INTRODUCTION	2
THE HISTORY OF THE BREED	2
DEVELOPMENT AND DISTRIBUTION	5
THE HISTORY OF THE AMERICAN SADDLEBRED IN GREAT BRITAIN	7
OFFICIAL BREED PROFILE	8
TEMPERAMENT	10
GAITS	11
SLOW-GAIT	11
RACK	11
A GUIDE TO SHOWING	12
FIVE-GAITED	12
THREE-GAITED	13
EQUITATION	13
FINE HARNESS	13
SHOW PLEASURE HARNESS	14
SHOWING IN BRITAIN	14
SADDLE SEAT	14
THE JOY OF SADDLEBREDS	16
VERSATILITY	20
ENTERTAINERS	20
THE HOLLYWOOD HORSE	21
FAMOUS DEVOTEES	22
CONCLUSION	23

INTRODUCTION

American Saddlebreds have a particular and fascinating history. Although their ancestry is British, credit for their sensational progression lies firmly with America.

Offering a riding experience that is quite extraordinary, thrilling and special, these multi-talented horses can apply their talented hooves, co-operative minds and uncanny intelligence to any task desired of them.

Bred for more than a century to be an efficient and comfortable ride, the American Saddlebred is considered to be the world's most highly adapted riding horse, and known by many affectionate epithets: peacock of the show ring, the Cadillac of horses; the society horse; the most beautiful horse in the world.

It has the distinction of having been the very first breed in America to have an established registry – the American Saddlebred Horse Association – formed in 1891, in Lexington, Kentucky. It is also America's national breed and arguably the USA's best kept secret.

THE HISTORY OF THE BREED

In the centuries before good roads were built, wheels were impracticable, and the best method of transportation was the riding horse. Those who could afford the luxury of choice invariably selected an ambler. These easy-gaited Hobbies and Galloways – named according to their region of origin but grouped together under the title of Old English Ambler – were favoured over trotting types. The ambler's four-beat gait (one foot on the ground at a time) provided a steady 'platform' on which to sit, devoid of both bump and roll, thus making riding a more pleasant experience. The bump of the trot was impossible for

infrequent riders, as was the side-to-side roll of the pace, and so the rapid gliding gait of the four-beat ambler solved many problems.

Kings, queens, pilgrims, clerics, lords and ladies, soldiers and generals all preferred these ambling horses, generically known as palfreys. The Wife of Bath rides one in Chaucer's *Canterbury Tales*; Queen Elizabeth I had a favourite palfrey and Mary Queen of Scots' palfrey was Black Agnes.

The improvement of roads facilitated the wheeled vehicle and gradually general-purpose riding horses became less vital. Thus the palfrey/ambler was replaced by cheaper trotting types and people and goods could be transported in carriages. Consigned to obscurity by the pressure of commerce, the ideal riding horse ultimately fell out of fashion, and slipped into extinction in Britain. Fortunately, however, some had been taken to the New World, settling in the Narragansett Bay region of Rhode Island, where, nurtured by the fresh waters and rich grass, they developed in stature and became known as Narragansett Pacers (made famous by Brown Beauty (right), the mount of Paul Revere for his heroic night gallop through the countryside to urge the Massachusetts colonists to resist the advance of the British troops).

Meanwhile, back in England, horse racing had become the fashion and a new breed had emerged. Amalgamating the remnants of the Old English Ambler with the newly imported Arabians, Turks and Barbs, led to the development of the English Thoroughbred – tall, fine, fast and, in many cases, retaining the ambler's gaits.

Inevitably, the new English Thoroughbred was also taken to America and soon Narragansett owners set about crossing their utilitarian mares with the fancy Thoroughbred stallions. By 1776 the resulting all-purpose generic 'American Horse' was so highly regarded that thereafter it was deliberately bred.

The new breed was able to trot like the Thoroughbred *and* amble like the old horses.

This made them prime utilitarian stock, useful in all aspects of human service. To this day they are popular with the Amish people for their stamina and amenability.

In the American Civil War, Saddlebreds were sought as mounts by the cavalry on both sides. Their smooth gaits meant officers and soldiers arrived at battle relatively fresh. General John Hunt Morgan and his raiders, mounted on Saddlebreds, passed into US legend for their great feats of endurance; he and General Nathan Forrest rode Saddlebreds exclusively. The breed was prized because it produced cavalry horses that displayed calm courage amid cannon fire and the melee of battle.

The years of war took an alarming toll and many excellent bloodlines were lost. But the survival of the breed can be credited to the opposing Generals. Robert E. Lee's principal request upon surrender was that his men should be allowed to keep their own horses. Appreciating that mostly these would be Saddlebreds like his own treasured Cincinatti, General Grant agreed. In retirement Lee continued to ride Traveller, saying, 'Traveller is my only companion, I may also say my pleasure. He and I, whenever practical, wander out in the mountains and enjoy sweet confidences.' When he died, some years after Lee, Traveller's skeleton was put on display in Virginia for people to view. It was eventually interred, and to this day tourists still toss coins on the headstone for good luck.

One of the gentleman breeders who helped found the breed association in 1891, General John B. Castleman, is honoured by a statue outside Cherokee Park in Lexington, mounted on his cherished Saddlebred mare, Carolina (below).

> **AUTHOR'S TIP**
>
> In historic documents, horses with ambling gaits were often called 'pacers' but in modern interpretations this has become inaccurate. Now a pacer literally means a horse that moves the legs on the same side in unison.

DEVELOPMENT AND DISTRIBUTION

The new breed, initially just called the Saddle Horse, was quickly appreciated by the horsemen of Kentucky and Missouri. They began a breeding programme to further improve its qualities. Initially, the ability to perform the saddle gaits was the principal criteria for registration. Inevitably some infusion experiments were carried out; in particular with Hackney blood and that of the fledgling Standardbred and Morgan Horse breeds. Ultimately the acknowledged foundation stallion was Gaines Denmark, a grandson of the imported Thoroughbred, Hedgeford, and out of an ambling mare.

As its fame spread rapidly across America, the breed was increasingly referred to as the American Saddle Horse. Meanwhile news of this fabulous new breed had travelled across the Atlantic to France, and a crafty bishop seeing a chance to curry favour, arranged for the shipment of one prime example as a gift for Marie Antoinette.

However, the general-sounding 'Saddle Horse' label, has led to much confusion for researchers in both American and equine history. The term 'saddle horse' written completely in lower case has been, understandably, misconstrued to

mean any horse trained to carry a saddle, but the adoption of the name Kentucky Saddler did little to change that. Thus, the identity of the breed, outside its own community, could have been easily lost.

In 1980 the name was formally confirmed as the American Saddlebred, but this did little to change the on-going effect of previous documentation.

Even now, there is a tendency to misrepresentation and the name often appears as 'American saddlebred' – giving the impression that it is not a specific breed but a generic reference to any American riding horse – or 'American saddle-bred' or just 'saddle bred'; but despite the changes, mistakes and inadvertent cloaking of his identity, the breed triumphs. Breeders and exhibitors throughout the States continue his development, and in a mechanized society the breed has a unique place as the world's most exciting and beautiful show horse.

During the late twentieth century, the Saddlebred's fame spread worldwide and the breed is soundly established in Canada, South Africa, Germany, Great Britain, Austria, Sweden, the Netherlands and Australia with individuals to be found in other European countries as well as Mexico and Haiti.

THE HISTORY OF THE AMERICAN SADDLEBRED IN GREAT BRITAIN

The first Saddlebreds found their way to Britain in the 1960s, when palomino stock was imported by two well-known breeders. These horses bred many palomino champions, bringing stature, quality and a good attitude to the golden horse. Many current-day palomino champions still carry some of the genes from this foundation stock. But with the ageing and eventual demise of this original stock, the gene pool became shallow.

In 1985 the American Saddlebred Association of Great Britain (ASAoGB) was formed in order to locate and register the living imports and their offspring before it was too late. It quickly became clear that if the Saddlebred was to thrive in this country, new imports had to be acquired and recognition of the breed had to be established.

The first horse to start this re-introduction campaign was Rare Visions (right), imported on 2nd May 1990. This five-gaited show mare was devoted to promoting her breed via demonstrations and displays.

Very soon, more pure-breds were being imported for breeding purposes, followed later by more performance horses. By 2004, the gene pool was out of the shallows with the importation of twenty-five pure-breds. General interest in the Saddlebred is growing monthly and the nucleus of devotees improving annually.

To reflect the re-introduction of the

descendants of the lost Old English Ambler, the ASAoGB's tag is 'Back to the Future' and, judging from the immense enthusiasm shown at displays, the future of America's best kept secret is bright.

There is a Saddlebred for every taste – he is truly a horse for all reasons.

OFFICIAL BREED PROFILE

The American Saddlebred carries himself with an attitude elusive of description – some call it class, presence, quality, style or charm. This superior air distinguishes his every movement.

The ideal American Saddlebred is well-proportioned and presents a beautiful overall picture. The animal should be in good flesh, with firm muscle tone and smooth, glossy coat. Masculinity in stallions and femininity in mares are important. The average height is 15–16 hh (153–163 cm) and the average weight 1,000–1,200 1b (440–540 k).

Head Well-shaped with large, wide-set expressive eyes, gracefully hooked ears set close together on top of the head and carried alertly; a clean smooth jaw line; a straight profile with a fine muzzle and large nostrils.

It is often said that a Saddlebred's muzzle should be fine enough to fit into a tea cup.

Neck Set at the very top of the shoulder, long, arched and well-flexed at the poll with a fine, clean throatlatch.

Withers Well-defined and prominent.

Shoulders Deep and sloping.

Back Strong and level with well-sprung ribs.

Croup Level.

Tail Tail comes out of the croup high. Tail-sets are traditional for show horses. It is considered that the upright profile of the tail aesthetically balances the upright carriage of the neck. The tail lowers again for regular use and retains complete mobility.

Legs The front legs should be set well forward under the shoulder. The line of the hind legs, in a natural stance, should be vertical from the point of the buttock to the back edge of the cannon bone. The forearms and hindquarters are well-muscled to the knees and hocks. The legs are straight with broad flat bone, sharply defined tendons and sloping pasterns.

Hooves Good and sound, open at the heel, neither toed-in nor toed-out.

Colours All colours are acceptable; those most prominent are chestnut (often with flaxen manes and tails), bay, brown and black, with grey, palomino and pinto (skewbald/piebald) being less common.

ASbd silhouette

TB silhouette

> **AUTHOR'S TIP**
>
> Good conformation is paramount, as with all breeds. But the word 'good' is relative to a standard and the Saddlebred sets its own exceedingly high standard, carrying forward the inherent ambling physique which has advanced and improved. He should be neither heavy nor weedy; but an elegant light horse. But this lightness is built on bone that, unlike the honeycombed bone of other breeds, is extremely dense, giving him a fundamental toughness.
>
> The Saddlebred's unique physique is the key to his eye-catching glamour; it is inappropriate to compare his outline to that of a familiar cob, Thoroughbred or Warmblood – he has a different genetic code (the ambling influence) and a different natural function.

TEMPERAMENT

It was not for nothing that both the ancient palfrey and the original Saddle Horse became generally popular; smooth comfortable gaits and smooth amenable temperaments are an irresistible combination producing highly trainable, versatile and usable animals for inexperienced or infrequent riders. Yet these tractable traits enhance rather than replace the stamina, courage, trainability, flair and glamour required by professional horsemen.

GAITS

All Saddlebreds perform the regular gaits of any ridden horse: walk, trot and canter. In addition, most Saddlebreds show a special aptitude for performing the gaits of their ambler ancestors; a genetic inheritance which is the result of the interaction of dominant and recessive genes (a subject beyond the scope of this book).

But do not be misled by the word 'ambler', it is a misnomer. The dictionary describes the amble as 'to walk at a leisurely relaxed pace'. This may well be how humans amble, but not the Saddlebred; for him the amble is rapid and ground-covering.

The two extra gaits are four-beat, that is to say there is only ever one foot in contact with the ground at a time.

SLOW-GAIT

This is a lateral gait: the left hind touches down an instant before the left fore; the left fore in turn lifts from the ground an instant before the right hind touches down, and so on. This eliminates the up-and-down movement associated with the trot and the side to side roll of the pace. Originally called the stepping pace, the peculiarly named slow-gait is not slow and, as the competitiveness of the show ring has increased over the years, has become fast; some say it has become too fast and has moved too far away from its original definition.

RACK

The rack (below), being neither lateral nor diagonal, falls midway between pace and trot with each leg flashing forward independently with an even 1-2-3-4 beat. It motors along at great speed with top horses travelling in excess of 35 mph (56 kph), even in the tight confines of an arena.

Performed with collection and animation, it should give the impression of serious intent to

AUTHOR'S TIP

It is important not to confuse ambling with pacing. As stated, in the pace, the hooves on the same side strike the ground in unison, and the pace is the speciality of the Saddlebred's close cousin, the harness-racing Standardbred.

get somewhere. All the energy of the motion is absorbed by the horse's body and the rapid square four-beat rhythm eliminates bump and roll. Because of the strength and stamina required to maintain the extra gaits in the highly animated form required in the show ring, the five-gaited show horse is often of slightly heavier build than the horses in the other divisions – a supreme athlete.

The five-gaited horse is also expected to perform a highly animated, collected and powerful trot, and a rhythmic smooth canter; as are the horses in the other divisions.

A GUIDE TO SHOWING

The Saddlebred has made showing into a sport. He is judged on motion, athleticism and presence in several divisions.

FIVE-GAITED

The five-gaited horse is the *crème de la crème* of the breed, and has to exhibit the three regular gaits of walk, trot and canter, plus the slow-gait and the rack (right). All gaits must be performed with energy and collection but in addition his rack should offer speed without loss of form. An animated expression is most

important since disinterest or robotic dullness will not win the coveted tricolour ribbon. He is shown with full mane and tail.

THREE-GAITED

The three-gaited horse performs just the walk, trot (right) and canter and all must be performed with collection, springy hocks and excellent knee action. The canter is a delightful 'rocking-chair' experience, slow and airy. Because speed is not demanded of them, they are required to be very elegant and light on the ground. The three-gaited horse is traditionally shown with a hogged mane because being usually of a lighter build than the five-gaited horse, the hogged mane is considered to show off the three-gaiter's swan neck.

EQUITATION

In this division it is not the horse that is judged but the rider. However, the horse is required to be presented in the Saddlebred style, showing elegance and motion as well as precision and obedience. Equitation horses are judged for their work on the rail, i.e. working against the fence of the arena, and are also required to perform a basic pattern test somewhat akin to preliminary dressage.

FINE HARNESS

The fine harness horse is shown in walk and trot and must exhibit animation, motion and brilliance. The vehicle used is a four-wheeled show wagon, similar to the English viceroy. Evening classes will see lady drivers dressed in amazing gowns as if driving themselves to a grand ball.

SHOW PLEASURE HARNESS

The horse performs in walk and trot again, with good manners being pre-eminent. The vehicle is usually a two-wheeled show sulky.

There are many variations within these divisions for 'high-octane' (top money winning) stakes horses, lady riders, professional trainers, juvenile horses, pleasure horses, amateur and junior riders. But in all divisions, performance is the most important thing; the horse must present his best Saddlebred motion, presence and flair.

SHOWING IN BRITAIN

The American Saddlebred Association of Great Britain (ASAoGB) holds classes that conform as closely as possible to the US requirements. However, in the interests of competition and filling classes, five-gaited horses are permitted to compete in three-gaited classes (without showing their extra gaits, of course). A lack of professional trainers in the UK means that as yet there cannot be trainers' classes or stakes classes, so the pleasure divisions are the order of the day.

Traditionally, the show Saddlebred is shown in the Saddle Seat style (see opposite). But to cater for the horses bred and raised in the UK, the ASAoGB supports traditional English hunter/riding horse classes for pure-breds and part-breds, together with side-saddle, western and colour classes.

The two shows held under the auspices of the ASAoGB are the British National Championships for the American Saddlebred Horse (established in 1997) and the American Classic, which caters for all American breeds.

Initially classes were established with the British Palomino Society and, more recently, the ASAoGB has worked with CHAPS (the Coloured Horse and Pony Society) and the Arab Horse Society to provide classes for part-bred Saddlebreds.

SADDLE SEAT

The traditional style of riding a Saddlebred is known to the Americans as the English style but it is also called Saddle Seat. A flat show saddle is used together with a double bridle dressed with a colourful patent leather cavesson and browband set. White girths are popular but, as with so many things, the colour of the girth is often also dictated by fashion.

The rider wears a saddle suit – i.e. a frock coat teamed with flared Kentucky jodhpurs, plus gloves, a colourful waistcoat, a tie or stock, and a soft bowler hat called a Derby – and is expected to be smart and clean.

This elegant attire is suited to both lady and gentleman riders and recalls the days of the gentry riding in the parks on Sunday.

The riding position is somewhat further back than the modern forward seat and is designed to place the rider over the Saddlebred's centre of gravity which – because of the upright neck, motion and general conformation – is correspondingly further back too.

This style of riding is also used with Tennessee Walking Horses and Morgan Horses, and has its own set of international competitions culminating in the Saddle Seat World Cup.

The Joy of Saddlebreds

The Joy of Saddlebreds • 17

18 • THE AMERICAN SADDLEBRED

VERSATILITY

The Saddlebred is not a one-talent horse. Whilst preserving and spectacularly demonstrating their unique heritage in the show ring, they bring to the modern day the qualities required of a sport horse – although it could be said that everything they attempt is carried out in their own inimitable style.

They have represented the USA in show jumping and eventing. Dressage comes easily to them as they are so instinctively in tune with collection and agile footwork; both pure-breds and part-breds easily master the *passage*.

Saddlebreds excel in endurance competitions (the World Champion for three consecutive years was a pure-bred gelding); and they delight in human company, which makes them ideal 'backyard' horses for general pleasure riding.

ENTERTAINERS

Saddlebreds have proved themselves in the circus, both from the High School aspect and as liberty horses. Katja Schumann was renowned for her High School performances on the British-bred palomino Saddlebred, Attila. In the early twentieth century, competitive High School classes were popular at horse shows in the USA and nearly all contestants were Saddlebreds, epitomized by the sensational pairing of Belle Beach and her trainer, the legendary Tom Bass. Bass was not only an exceptionally fine trainer, but was also black, which, for the time, made him unusual as well as exceptional.

Showmen of all types have used Saddlebreds in the past; Buffalo Bill (William F. Cody) perhaps being the most famous, and the principal horse in his Wild West Show, the grey Columbus, had also originally been trained by Tom Bass.

Mr Rythm [sic] was bred and trained by Darrell Wallen: 'I intended him as a show horse and started to gait him, but he told me that he would rather be a High School horse, so we set to work and within six weeks he had learned more than fifty-five different manoeuvres. He was one in a million.' His repertoire involved more than sixty 'High School' movements including the traditional Spanish Walk and, more exotically, dancing the hula (wearing a grass skirt); he'd even sway with the rhythm of a waltz tune; walk on his knees, and rear on command. He holds the world record for walking on his back legs having covered an amazing 355 ft (108 m), and he would happily ride a see-saw, count, trot on the spot and canter backwards. All solely on voice command.

In the 1920s another notable Saddlebred, aptly named Two-Step, was even trained to roller-skate.

THE HOLLYWOOD HORSE

Many Saddlebreds are used in the film world because they are beautiful, elegant and very easy to train, remaining unflustered by the 'on-off' demands and general chaos of a film set.

They have enjoyed international popularity on the large and small screen as Fury, Black Beauty and the talking horse Mr Ed, whose television show won the Golden Globe as Best TV Show in 1963. Highland Dale, who played Fury and Black Beauty, earned over half a million dollars during his career, second only to Lassie as the highest-paid animal in Hollywood. Highland Dale starred in major movies alongside many celebrities: *Riding High* with Bing Crosby; *Giant* with Rock Hudson, James Dean and Elizabeth Taylor; and *Black Gold* with Anthony Quinn and Katherine De Mille. In the latter film Highland Dale took three roles: Black Gold himself, and Black Gold's sire and dam!

Ralph McCutcheon, who trained Highland Dale, and who has worked with many other breeds, is on record as saying that Saddlebreds are unusually easy to train, beautiful, adaptable and he has used them to play Thoroughbred Kentucky Derby winners and harness racing champions, because they have the looks that an audience imagines big race winners would have.

Amongst his many other films, Saddlebred Black Diamond played in *Zorro*, and Disney's horsemaster for this film remarked that he was

the most versatile actor he had worked with and never needed a double for tricks or stunts.

Saddlebreds have also appeared in *Gone With The Wind*, *Gettysburg*, *Star Trek-Generations*, and many Westerns.

There are few aspects of equine activity where this breed's intelligent tractability and superb athleticism have not permitted him to try and triumph.

Saddlebreds have worked the cattle herds alongside the more traditional stock horse, the Quarter Horse, with skill and 'savvy'; they helped pioneer the West; worked the cotton plantations; raced with the master on Saturdays and ferried the family to church on Sundays.

Famous Devotees

In the late nineteenth century, a sensational show horse, the coal-black stallion Rex McDonald, was idolized by the public and was also visited by US Presidents.

Franklin D. Roosevelt loved to spend time with his Saddlebred, New Deal; Ronald Reagan owned Wills Fancy and Callaways Nancy D; and Harry Truman was the proud possessor of Johnson's King.

General Robert E. Lee's Saddlebred Traveller (below) was also the eponymous hero in Richard Adams' best-selling novel.

The sons of outlaw Jessie James's mare were registered by the descendant of an original member of the James-Younger gang.

Currently, one well-known breeder and exhibitor of American Saddlebreds is the actor William Shatner (right). His most famous horses include Sultan's Great Day; Great Belles of Fire; Eleanor Rigby; Call Me Ringo.

CONCLUSION

The Saddlebred is the horse of dreams, a horse of history, and the horse of the future. He preserves all that was best about the ancient horses and has been developed as a superlative breed for any occasion or reason. Whilst essentially a gaited breed he offers a trot that is second-to-none thereby widening his scope to any sport or discipline required of him. Experts have remarked that he is probably 'the world's most overlooked ideal dressage and pleasure horse'.

He is a special breed, with the ability to integrate without losing his own unique style.

ACKNOWLEDGEMENTS

I would like to thank the following for supplying photographs for this book: *Saddle & Bridle* magazine; Main Event Photography; Doug Shiflet Photographic; Stuart Vestey Photography; Jamie Donaldson; Howard Schatzburg; Darrel Wallen; Dr. S. Raun; Maggie Van Meter; Janet Browne; Linda Colquhoun; Jane A. Green; the Rt. Hon. Lord Denis Healey of Riddlesden; Samantha Hullis; Sue Lea; Robin Neal; Mick Pickford; Washington & Lee University; Michael Miley.

British Library Cataloguing-in-Publication Data.
A catalogue record for this book is available from the British Library

ISBN-10: 0-85131-910-6
ISBN-13: 978-0-85131-910-0

© Cheryl R. Lutring 2005

Cheryl R. Lutring asserts her right to be identified
as the author of this work in accordance with the Copyright,
Design and Patent Act 1988

No part of this book may be reproduced, stored in a retrieval system,
or transmitted, in any form or by any means, electronic, mechanical,
photocopying, recording or otherwise, without the prior permission
of the publisher. All rights reserved.

Published in Great Britain in 2005 by
J. A. Allen an imprint of Robert Hale Ltd.,
Clerkenwell House, 45–47 Clerkenwell Green,
London EC1R 0HT

Design and Typesetting by Paul Saunders
Series editor Jane Lake
Printed by Gutenberg Press Limited, Malta